RAILS AROUND PRESTON

MIKE RHODES

AMBERLEY

First published 2025

Amberley Publishing
The Hill, Stroud
Gloucestershire, GL5 4EP

www.amberley-books.com

Copyright © Mike Rhodes, 2025

The right of Mike Rhodes to be identified as
the Author of this work has been asserted in
accordance with the Copyrights, Designs and
Patents Act 1988.

ISBN 978 1 3981 1869 0 (print)
ISBN 978 1 3981 1870 6 (ebook)

British Library Cataloguing in Publication Data.
A catalogue record for this book is available from
the British Library.

Origination by Amberley Publishing.
Printed in the UK.

Abbreviations

AC	Alternating Current	LNER	London North Eastern Railway
APT	Advanced Passenger Train	LNWR	London North Western Railway
B&PR	Blackburn & Preston Railway	LO&PR	Liverpool Ormskirk & Preston
BNFL	British Nuclear Fuels Ltd		Railway
BOL&PR	Bolton & Preston Railway	MPD	Motive Power Depot
BR	British Rail	NMT	New Measurement Train
BRCW	Birmingham Railway Carriage &	NRM	National Railway Museum
	Wagon Co.	NSE	Network South East
BREL	British Rail Engineering Ltd	NUR	North Union Railway
CAF	Construcciones y Auxiliar de	P&LR	Preston & Lancaster Railway
	Ferrocarriles	P&WJR	Preston & Wyre Joint Railway
DMU	Diesel Multiple Unit	PC	Preston Corporation
DRS	Direct Rail Services	RCTS	Railway Correspondence & Travel
DVT	Driving Van Trailer		Society
ECML	East Coast Main Line	RES	Rail Express Systems
ECS	Empty Coaching Stock	ROF	Royal Ordnance Factory
ELPR	East Lancashire Preservation Railway	S&C	Settle & Carlisle Railway
ELR	East Lancashire Railway	SLOA	Steam Locomotive Owners
EMR	East Midlands Railway		Association
EMU	Electric Multiple Unit	SLS	Stephenson Locomotive Society
EWS	English Welsh & Scottish Railway	SO	Saturdays Only
GBRF	GB Railfreight Ltd	SR	Southern Railway
GNER	Great North Eastern Railway	SuO	Sundays Only
GWR	Great Western Railway	TMD	Traction Motive Power Depot
HST	High Speed Train	UCLAN	University of Central
L&PJR	Lancaster & Preston Junction		Lancashire
	Railway	WCML	West Coast Main Line
LCGB	Locomotive Club of Great Britain	WD	War Department
LMR	London Midland Region	WLR	West Lancashire Railway
LMS	London Midland & Scottish	WO	Wednesdays Only
	Railway	WR	Western Region

Note:
p. 68, 1. Source: Article by Robin Bamber, Pt 1, *The Preston Magazine*, Issue 21.

Introduction

The first layout of Preston station was opened in October 1838 when the North Union Railway (NUR) laid a line connecting Wigan and Preston. There were just five platforms with two tracks extending at the north end under Fishergate. During the next decade further lines converged on Preston from Longridge (P&LR), Lancaster (L&PJR) and Fleetwood (P&WJR) in 1840, Bolton (BOL&PR) in 1843, Blackburn (B&PR) in 1846 (absorbed by the ELR) and Ormskirk/Liverpool (LO&PR) in 1849. By 1850 the original station was totally inadequate for the number of trains using it and the ELR (1845–59) was being charged extortionate rates for its trains to travel on the NUR from Farington and consequently built its own station (Butler Street) on the east side of the NUR station, which had three bay platforms and one through line which joined the NUR at the south end. These platforms were accessed by a newly constructed line from Bamber Bridge/Lostock Hall and catered for trains from East Lancashire/Yorkshire and West Lancashire. It also entailed the construction of a new bridge, which carried two tracks over the River Ribble. The NUR had also created a single line in 1846, which diverged alongside the station and proceeded at a falling gradient of 1 in 29 towards the river and served the then berthing facility of Victoria Quay.

By the mid-1870s it was realised that the current station was not fit for purpose and plans were drawn up for a complete rebuild, which included the provision of more platforms and an increased number of approach tracks from the south across Union Bridge. The new station was brought into full use in July 1880 and had seven through platforms and five bay platforms and the general layout from that time forms the nucleus of today's station. The West Lancashire Railway (WLR) opened a line from Southport in 1878 and for a period (1882–1900) used its own station at the foot of Fishergate Hill. In July 1896 there was a serious accident north of the station and this prompted a rethink of the design layout at the north end. Partly in consequence, the station was enlarged on the west side, which required the acquisition of adjacent land, including Harding's horse tram depot and stables. Fishergate Bridge was widened and two new platforms were constructed either side of an island; the work was completed in early 1903. Two further approach tracks were laid across the river, bringing the total to seven. The station reached its maximum size in 1913 when another through platform (originally numbered 10 but later altered to 13) was added on the East Lancashire side.

Signifying the importance of Preston's role in local industry, there were a number of goods facilities within the town environs and nearby. These comprised Butler Street Goods Depot, Cattle Market Sidings, Christian Road Goods Depot, Deepdale Coal Depot, Dock Street Coal Sidings, Greenbank Goods Station, Ladywell Sidings (serving the canal wharves), Maudland Goods Depot, North Union Sidings, Ribble Sidings and the West Lancashire Goods Station, while a short distance to the south were Farington and Lostock Hall Sidings and Carriage Shed, all of which have since been closed. In addition the dock complex had opened in 1892 and eventually contained over 26 miles of railway, which were worked by its own fleet of small shunting engines. A later addition was that of the Royal Ordnance Factory complex at Euxton, which contained a number of sidings and its own station platforms on the main railway line.

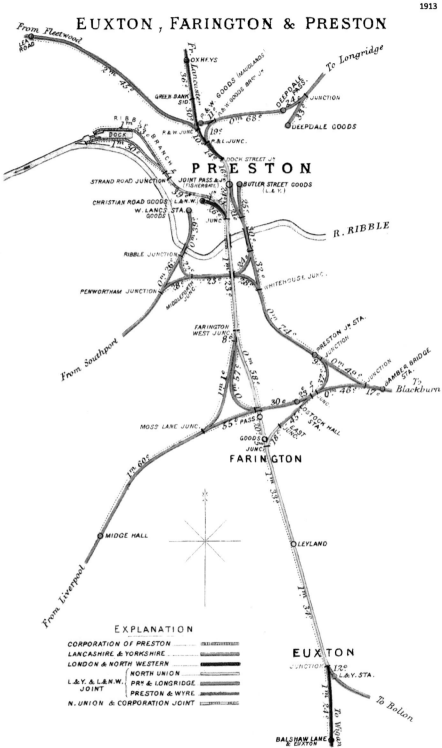

1913

EUXTON, FARINGTON & PRESTON

Steam engine sheds were located on the west side at Maudland, coded 10B (later 24K), and at nearby Lostock Hall, coded 24C (10D). In 2024 the only siding space in use comprised the relaid Ladywell engineer's sidings on the east side and the various lines for stabling multiple units on the west side (Croft Street and Pitt Street), all to the north of Fishergate Bridge.

Passenger trains to Longridge were withdrawn in 1930 with the closure of Deepdale, Ribbleton and Grimsargh stations, although the full length of the line saw freight activity until November 1967. Trains continued to serve the Courtauld's Rayon manufacturing factory at Ribbleton until 1980 and thereafter coal traffic continued to run to the Deepdale Depot, latterly from South Wales, until 1994.

On 28 June 1960 a disastrous fire at Preston engine shed totally destroyed the roof and a number of engines were badly damaged. Despite soldiering on for another fifteen months, the shed was closed as an operational base in September 1961 but was used for the storage of withdrawn engines for a few more years after that, the most notable of which was Coronation Class Pacific No. 46257 *City of Salford*, which had been condemned in September 1964 and was noted on shed on 28 December while on its way to Arnott Young's scrapyard at Troon for cutting up. Later that decade the four-track section of the Blackpool line from Maudland to Kirkham was reduced to two tracks following the 1966 summer holiday season and the slow lines on the WCML, which had extended from Oxheys to Barton, were taken out of use and lifted in 1969, although passing loops at Barton (northbound) and Oxheys (southbound) were provided.

On 7 September 1964 the line to Southport was closed in its entirety with the loss of nine more stations. Through trains to Liverpool via Ormskirk ceased to run in May 1970 with such a journey now requiring a change of train at Ormskirk, a practice that still prevails today. Later the same year platforms 1 and 2 were taken out of passenger use and reutilised for the reception of mail/parcels trains. The connecting footbridge from platform 3 was removed and the island platform was then extended beyond Fishergate Bridge in the following year. The one remaining through platform (formerly number 2) now sees very little use. Following these alterations the remaining platforms were renumbered.

Following authorisation to continue the electrification of the WCML north of Weaver Junction the station underwent a substantial reconfiguration in 1971–73. The work included closing the East Lancashire side of the station (no more would holidaymakers from Scotland and the North East be confused by passing through Preston station twice) in its entirety, followed by a complete resignalling scheme whereby all seven of the mechanical signal boxes in the vicinity of the station and other nearby boxes were closed and done away with. The new colour-light signals were henceforth controlled from Preston's new Power Signal Box, which was built on the site of the former steam shed and was officially opened by HM Queen Elizabeth II on 7 May 1974. On completion of the works the station then had six through platforms available for passenger traffic and two bay platforms, with three other through lines.

 Continuing the retraction, Preston Docks was officially closed in October 1981 following a gradual period of decline. Few changes have taken place since other than the redevelopment of the land on the East Lancashire side, latterly with the addition of a multistorey car park for railway patrons, which opened in 2009, and extensive renovation and maintenance works to the Grade II listed building, particularly to the station roof canopies. Electrification of the lines to Blackpool and Manchester was finally achieved in 2018 and 2019, respectively.

At the start of the 1960s most of the prestigious express trains such as The Caledonian, Mid-day Scot and Royal Scot were still in the hands of the Coronation and Princess Royal Class Pacifics, with Jubilees, Patriots and Royal Scots also to be seen in significant numbers on other passenger turns. Local passenger trains were generally worked by Fairburn- and Stanier-designed Tank engines. Unfitted freight trains were to be seen behind a mixed bag of locomotives including 8Fs,

9Fs, Black 5s, Crabs, Midland 0-6-0s, WDs and various Standard types. All this activity could be viewed from the famous, or should that be infamous, 'Glass Bridge', which was legendary among local spotters. Preston shed had a small allocation of Jinties which were used for shunting work in the various yards; these were transferred to Lostock Hall following the closure of Preston shed. Of special note was a small allocation of ex-LNWR 0-8-0 Super Ds, which could often be seen powering up the dock incline on local trip freights, and two Kitson 0-4-0 saddle tank engines, which were required to work the tight radius curves at Greenbank Sidings.

Throughout the decade steam gradually began to diminish, although with the reallocation of most of the Britannia Pacifics to the two Carlisle sheds in the early part of the 1960s they could be seen in abundance at Preston, particularly throughout 1965. Another type to appear in the area was the Ivatt 2-6-0, a number of which gravitated to Lostock Hall and among other duties were used to steam heat the sleeping cars which were detached from the Euston to Barrow mail train at Preston. Gradually diesels began to take over with English Electric Class 40 Type 4s and the somewhat unreliable Metrovic Class 28 Type 2s a common sight in the area. Excursion traffic to Blackpool saw a wide variety of steam types, particularly from the Midlands and Yorkshire, pass through the station. Most notable were the appearances of A4 No. 60022 *Mallard* on 30 September 1961 and of A1 No. 60114 *W P Allen* on 28 September 1963. Ex-LNER B1s could be seen in abundance on special trains from the Yorkshire Woollen towns to Blackpool. In addition, A1 No. 60131 *Osprey* also made a rare appearance at Lostock Hall when it arrived on 2 August 1964 with an ECS train and returned north a couple of days later at the head of the 'Lakes Express'. A2 No. 60528 *Tudor Minstrel* was another Gresley Pacific that put in an appearance at Preston when it hauled a railtour from Manchester Exchange to Edinburgh Waverley on 23 April 1966. Somewhat significantly, the area hosted the last regular steam workings in the country and these finished on 3 August 1968. Towards the end of the decade excursion traffic had reduced considerably and Classes 24/5, 31, 37, 40, 45 and 47 had become the order of the day.

A wide variety of diesel and electric types have regularly graced the station together with innumerable one-off visits from unusual preserved classes, both steam and diesel. The appearance of new Brush Type 4 D1551 working under headcode 1Z49 on 25 January 1964 heralded the start of a long programme of test runs of new Class 47s from Crewe Works (the last to be recorded was D1111 on 7 February 1967). In 1966 pairs of Class 20s based at Polmadie could be seen regularly hauling loaded trains of cartics between Morris Cowley and Bathgate. Also that year new Class 20s, built at nearby Vulcan Foundry, made regular appearances working north on test trains under headcode 1T60 (later also used by Class 50s on test). February 1968 brought the first appearance of a Class 50, a type that had a six-year spell working many of the Anglo-Scottish trains, often in multiple, until full electrification of the line was commissioned in May 1974. Later that same year Class 17 Clayton Type 1s, a number of which were then based at Carnforth, regularly appeared in pairs on a Preston to Barrow parcels working (3P24). All the early types of electrics could then be seen at Preston including the newly introduced Class 87s, which were later followed by the Class 90s, in 1989. It should be noted that examples of Classes 89, 91 and 92 have also been recorded at Preston. The former was hauling a test train which followed a long tradition of one-off locomotives hauling such trains through Preston – viz Nos 10000/1, DP2, GT3 and DELTIC in much earlier years.

The electric locomotives held sway for more than two decades. Rail privatisation was implemented in April 1994 and the WCML franchise was awarded to Virgin Trains, which commenced operation of services through Preston on 9 March 1997. Sir Richard Branson gradually introduced a new fleet of trains on the west coast route consisting of Class 221 Voyager diesel and Class 390 Pendolino electric units, which displaced all the loco-hauled trains over time. The Pendolinos passed to new franchise operator Avanti West Coast in December 2019.

Many different types of diesel locomotives have been seen on regular freight diagrams over the years and these are too numerous to list, although one such train which ran for several decades was the Lanfina Tar Distillers' tanker train from the Lindsey Refinery on South Humberside (origin transferred to Teesside in 2023) to Preston Docks, which operated for the last time in October 2024. A wide variety of both first- and second-generation diesel and electric multiple units have also maintained the local services during the period under review.

At the turn of the nineteenth century there were around seventy stations within a 15-mile radius of Preston; 120 years later the total had all but halved. Standing sentry over all this activity, to the immediate north of the station, is St Walburge's Church, which was completed in 1854 and has a spire that stands at 309 feet tall (the third highest in the UK). The author has been recording railway activity in the area for over sixty years and this account is based on his notes and observations. Special thanks go to Martyn Hilbert for the use of some of his images.

Mike Rhodes

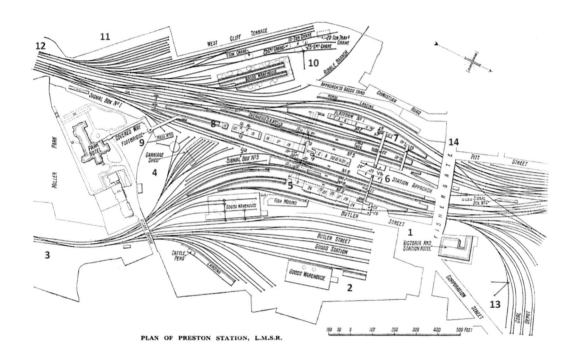

PLAN OF PRESTON STATION, L.M.S.R.

Preston station layout, 1913–71: 1. Butler Street entrance (East Lancs). 2. Butler Street Goods Depot. 3. East Lancs Bridge over the river. 4. East Lancs Engine and Carriage Sidings including a small turntable. 5. ELR platforms. 6. Main entrance (North Union). 7. Additional platforms numbered 1 and 2. 8. South-end bay platforms 5A and 6A (renumbered 3C and 4C *c.* 1971). 9. 'Glass Bridge' to the Park Hotel. 10. Christian Road Goods Depot. 11. North Union Sidings. 12. North Union Bridge (widened to seven tracks). 13. Dock Street Coal Sidings. 14. Fishergate Bridge (built *c.* 1875 and widened in 1901–02).

Stanier 8F 2-8-0 No. 48471 of Newton Heath Shed is seen on the northbound through goods line on the widened section on 16 September 1967 with a train of empty track panel bolster wagons, and is probably returning the wagons from the Castleton Engineering Depot to Workington Steel. Behind is Christian Road Goods Depot and No. 2A Signal Box. The box straddles the single-line dock branch and was opened in July 1900 and closed on 16 May 1971. The Swindon-built 8F was withdrawn w/e 27 April 1968.

Lostock Hall Black 5 No. 45212 has just left Ribble Sidings on 23 March 1968 with 7P11, the 10.55 to Heysham Harbour, with a mixed consist of four-wheeled wagons. It is again seen on the Down goods line and is about to blast under Fishergate Bridge. A lone Class 47 and a Class 08 diesel shunter can be seen in Pitt Street Sidings. This loco is now preserved.

Platforms 1 and 2 were taken out of passenger use in 1971 along with the through goods lines. The island platform was extended under Fishergate Bridge and three short stabling roads were provided on the west side. Class 47 No. 47701 (D1932) in RES livery is seen alongside what was platform 1 on 15 January 1994. Built at the Brush Works in February 1966, it lasted in service until December 2003. This loco is also now preserved.

Looking north at the parcels sidings with Class 47 No. 47824 (D1780) and single unit Class 153 Sprinter No. 153333 on 22 February 1992. The unit had not long returned from Hunslet Barclay at Kilmarnock after conversion from a Class 155. It was still in service in 2023 as part of the Transport for Wales fleet.

Somewhat unusual at Preston was former 1963 York-built Clacton Class 309 EMU No. 309617, seen in the parcels platform on 1 October 1994. These units finished on the Great Eastern in January 1994 and seven sets were placed in store at Blackpool North. They then entered service from Longsight TMD in Manchester from where they worked local trains until May 2000. This unit was scrapped at Eastleigh in 2004.

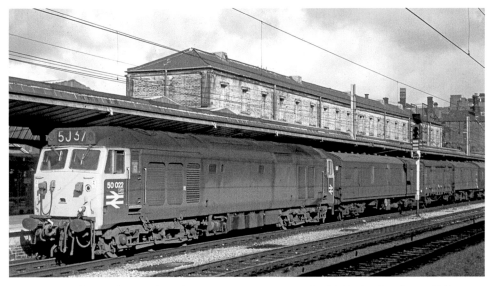

The author's first sighting of a Class 50 at Preston was of D405 in Butler Street Sidings on 19 February 1968. Thereafter they became a common sight for the next seven to eight years, working most of the WCML expresses until the electrification was fully energised. In this undated picture No. 50022 (D422) is seen under the wires at the parcels platform with 5J37 Barrow to Manchester Red Bank Parcels. It was transferred to Bristol Bath Road TMD in March 1976 and withdrawn in September 1988. (KDH Archive)

Much more unusual at Preston was the sight of a Class 26, although they did have a regular working for a short period of time. Allocated to Eastfield MPD (Scottie Dog emblem), No. 26031 (D5331) was in charge of the WO Carlisle to Preston Parcels on 24 May 1989. Built at the BRCW Company in June 1959, the Type 2 was withdrawn later in the year and cut up at M. C. Metals of Springburn the following year.

Over the weekend of 24–25 February 1990 the east-side platforms were closed for engineering works. The Class 87s were introduced to the WCML on a regular basis from late 1973, taking over the full schedule of trains, along with the Class 85s and 86/2s, the following May. No. 87014 *Knight of the Thistle*, since repainted into InterCity livery, is unusually seen at platform 1 with 1S59 07.35 London Euston to Inverness Clansman on Saturday 24th.

Seen from a similar vantage point on 4 May 1968 is Stanier Black 5 No. 44950 (10D) shunting parcels vans for 3P24, the 09.58 Preston to Barrow Parcels. No. 44950 was built at Horwich in March 1946 and continued in service until the end of steam. Following steam's demise this train was then worked for a number of months by pairs of Clayton Type 1 centre-cabs from the early D85xx series, a number of which were then based at Carnforth, although most of them didn't see the year out.

Sprinter Class 150/2 DMU No. 156413 is standing at the old platform 2 (through parcels platform) on 24 February 1990 with the 09.45 Hazel Grove to Blackpool North. These units were built by Metro-Cammell in 1987–89. No. 156413 was part of the East Midlands Train fleet in 2022.

The DMU unit that kick-started the so-called Pacer revolution. No. 140001 was a prototype two-car DMU, which was built at Derby's Litchurch Lane Works and was trialled in the early 1980s in various parts of the country. It is seen in platform 1 on 30 September 1981 waiting to depart with the 07.50 branch-line service to Ormskirk. It is now preserved.

The Class 158 was originally referred to as a Super Sprinter but the name didn't stick for long. There were 182 sets originally built at the BREL Works at Derby between 1989 and 1992 and these comprised seventeen three-car and 165 two-car sets. The final ten sets were operated by the West Yorkshire Passenger Transport Executive and were originally painted red and cream. Former Metro-liveried No. 158903 is seen departing platform 1 with a York/ Leeds to Blackpool North service on 26 July 2010.

One of the more unusual types of DMU to have regular diagrams through Preston was the Class 180 Adelante unit. Three sets were leased to Northern Rail and based at Newton Heath TMD between December 2008 and November 2011. No. 180103 waits at platform 3 with a Blackpool North to Manchester Victoria working on an unrecorded date.

The splendid signal gantry at the north end is viewed from a carriage in the consist of the RCTS Lancastrian Railtour No. 2, which ran on 20 April 1968, as the train approaches the station behind Britannia 4-6-2 No. 70013 *Oliver Cromwell* on the Fleetwood to Windermere leg of the tour. Black 5 4-6-0 No. 45156 *Ayrshire Yeomanry* (8A) had run back from Fleetwood light engine ahead of the tour and would next proceed to Morecambe. Two Class 24s can be seen stabled in Pitt Street Sidings. The signal gantry disappeared under the 1971–73 station remodelling/resignalling scheme.

An unusual collection of units was present in Croft Street Sidings on 28 August 1988. From the left is fairly new Class 156 No. 156430, Newton Heath Class 104 set N677 (Nos 53434 and 53507) and Tyseley's Class 117 set T309 (Nos 51372, 59490 and 51414), with the latter having arrived on a special working. (Martyn Hilbert)

Two pictures taken from the same vantage point at Maudland on 6 July 1985. *Above:* Class 37 No. 37042 (D6742) is seen negotiating the reverse curve at the head of 1S91, the 09.45 SO Blackpool North to Stranraer. This was the return working of 1M17, which departed Stranraer at 01.30. The train changed locomotives twice at both Preston and Carlisle. Withdrawn in 2007, the Type 3 is now preserved at the Eden Valley Railway and is based at Warcop. *Below:* The BRCW Class 110 DMU was introduced in 1961 and the first twenty sets were initially based at Bradford Hammerton Street MPD to work services across the Pennines via the Calder Valley route to Manchester and Blackpool. Ten further sets were allocated to Newton Heath the following year. An unidentified set is seen leading the 12.25 Blackpool North to Manchester Victoria. The type lasted in service until 1990. The Grade II listed St Mark's Church (built in 1862–63 and now housing residential flats) is prominent in the background, while St Walburge's is just off camera to the right.

A view taken from part way up St Walburge's 309-feet-tall church spire, looking south towards the station on 25 July 2009. On the left a Class 185 DMU is heading north with a train for Windermere. In the centre a Class 142 can be seen curving to the right with a train for Blackpool South, while a Class 156 rests in Croft Street Sidings. The power box is on the right and occupies part of the former steam shed site. (Martyn Hilbert)

Class 31s No. 31427 (D5618) and No. 31413 (D5812) *Severn Valley Railway* approach Preston with the 07.06 Blackpool North to Manchester Victoria 'Club Train' on 7 July 1992. When allocated to Tinsley TMD in the early 1960s D5812 would have most likely worked to Blackpool on an excursion. St Mark's Church can be seen in the background.

Class 20s were never a common sight at Preston. Locomotives based at Polmadie could be seen in pairs at the head of car trains on the WCML in the mid-1960s but it would be the late 1980s before they again emerged on a regular basis when Wigan MPD provided the type to work engineer's trains in the area. Nos 20040 (D8040) and 20129 (D8129) are seen at Maudland on 18 March 1990 with a mixed rake of Metro-Cammell-built Catfish/Dogfish empty spoil wagons from Kirkham tip.

Rose Grove's Stanier 8F 2-8-0 No. 48423 is seen drifting off Maudland Viaduct on 18 April 1968 with train 7P80, the 14.10 Wyre Dock to Burnley Central. There are at least six chimneys visible from the mills in the Ashton and Tulketh districts of the town. The photographer's vantage point is adjacent to Maudland Viaduct Signal Box. The 8F remained in service until the last day of steam operation having completed nearly twenty-five years' service with the LMS/BR.

An unidentified Swindon-built cross-country Class 120 DMU coupled to a Class 104 is seen crossing the ten-arch brick Maudland Viaduct with a train for Blackpool North on 19 May 1982. The terraced houses/shops which stood in the foreground had been demolished to facilitate the widening of Water Lane. The original bridge was of a twelve-arch construction and only carried one track. The present bridge was built in 1846 with two tracks and then widened on each side to carry four tracks in 1888/9. Maudland Viaduct Signal Box, which closed on 4 February 1973, was situated just to the right. The Rhodes (no relation) carpet store, visible through the arches, was still trading in 2024.

The low-headroom cast-iron girder bridge spanning Waterloo Road at the junction of Tulketh Brow had claimed a number of corporation buses' roofs over the years. Across the extended weekend of 28–30 August 1984 the nearly 100-year-old bridge was replaced with a new reinforced concrete-beam structure. The work required the total closure of the railway line and the adjacent roads. Cutting with acetylene torches is well underway in this view recorded on 28 April. The line reopened on the 31st.

Another view of the Waterloo Road Bridge works as seen from St Mark's Road. The bridge was located immediately north of Maudland Viaduct. Split-headcode Class 40 No. 40129 (D329) is seen in attendance with sundry wagons stabled on the adjacent track. The wide expanse shows where the other two tracks used to stand. The new bridge only catered for the remaining two tracks. The Type 4 was withdrawn a month later and cut up in August.

Type 4 Co-Co No. 45007 (D119) is seen rounding the curve at Ashton with Blackpool Road Bridge (A5085) in the background; this picture predates the construction of Tom Benson Way. The Peak is working 1N79 the 15.05 SO Blackpool North to Newcastle Central, which would have travelled via Manchester. This was the return of 1M66 that departed Newcastle at 07.10. Class 45 No. 45007 was withdrawn in July 1988 and eventually scrapped in November 1992.

The view from Blackpool Road (A5085) Bridge looking towards Preston. Black 5 4-6-0 No. 44942 (10D) is in charge of 1P42, the 12.44 Preston to Blackpool South. This train originated at London Euston and split at Preston, with the other portion destined for Windermere. The Horwich-built loco was withdrawn w/e 22 June. The adjacent tracks had only been removed some eighteen or so months previously.

Preserved Thompson B1 4-6-0 No. 61264 is seen at the same location some thirty-seven years later, on 5 November 2005, with a Cleethorpes to Blackpool North special working. Withdrawn on 21 November 1965, the B1 had a short spell as a stationary boiler before being sold to Woodham's at Barry from where it was rescued in 1976. It was awaiting overhaul at the Nottingham Heritage Railway in 2024. A B1 rounding the curve was a common sight on summer Saturdays during the 1950s and early 1960s.

A third view at the same location without the addition of a smoke screen. GBRF Class 66 No. 66754 *Northampton Saints* (with No. 66760 *Gordon Harris* on the rear) was photographed with special train 1Z24 Doncaster to Blackpool North on 30 July 2016. The 66 entered service in 2014. Tom Benson Way is on the left.

First-generation Derby Lightweight (aluminium) Class 108 DMU Nos 51931 and 51571 pass under Blackpool Road Bridge with a train from Blackpool North to Liverpool Lime Street on 9 July 1985. The bridge was in the process of being widened to accommodate a new road, which was being constructed partly on what used to be railway land (two removed tracks) and partly on land annexed from the adjacent Haslam Park. The roadway was named Tom Benson Way after a local record-breaking long-distance walker.

A view from the road bridge looking towards Lea sees Stanier 8F 2-8-0 No. 48167 of Rose Grove Shed on 5 June 1968 in charge of 7P80, the 14.10 Wyre Dock to Burnley Central coal empties. The 8F was built at Crewe for the LMS as No. 8167 in April 1943; it was withdrawn on 3 August 1968. The two tracks were lifted in late 1966. Ashton Signal Box (1879) can just be seen in the far distance on the right; it was closed on 4 February 1973.

From the exact same viewpoint on 15 September 1991 Class 47 No. 47509 (D1953) was photographed in charge of the 15.26 Blackpool North to London Euston. The Type 4 was turned out from the Brush Works in November 1966, nearly two years before the 8F was withdrawn, and was taken out of service just a year after this picture was recorded. The 47 would have been replaced by an electric loco at Preston.

A somewhat substandard picture but nonetheless of historical value. B1 4-6-0s No. 61173 and No. 61024 *Addax*, both of which were allocated to Wakefield Shed (56A) at the time, are seen alongside Haslam Park with an excursion from Yorkshire to Blackpool North on 5 June 1965. When the line was widened to four tracks the two extra tracks carried trains in each direction, meaning that tracks one and three were for Down trains and tracks two and four carried trains towards Preston. You can almost smell the smoke.

Taken from close to Ashton Signal Box on 10 April 1968, Stanier 8F No. 48062 of 10F hurries past the photographer with 8P19 from Burnley Central to Burn Naze with a consist of coal for the Ammonia Soda Works. The loco was built at Vulcan Foundry in November 1936 and lasted in service until the end of steam. The houses on the right were relatively new at the time and are situated in West Park Avenue.

Taken from almost the same location but looking in the opposite direction (from the vantage point of Tom Benson Way) some twenty-four years later is Class 37 No. 37426 (D6999) with the 06.50 Blackpool North to Liverpool Lime Street so-called 'Club Train'. The name was revived from the steam days of the old LMS which back in the day was bestowed upon certain upmarket trains for the landed gentry, which, among other routes, ran between Manchester and Southport/ Blackpool and Liverpool and Blackpool.

Class 40s were a common sight on the Midland Region (MR) for some two-and-a-half decades. Seen during their closing years at Lea (Sidgreaves Lane) on 1 August 1981 is No. 40082 (D282) with an unidentified train bound for Blackpool. Tulketh Mill is visible on the skyline (centre). Lea Road station was situated on the bend at the rear of the train; it was opened in 1842 and closed on 2 May 1938, although the one island platform (minus buildings) was still extant in 1968. Both Salwick and Kirkham stations also only had one island platform, with none being provided on the widened lines. The land on the left will hopefully see the construction of a new station named Cottam in the not-too-distant future. At the time of writing the proposal had reached the contract letting stage with funding already in place.

Above: Seen at speed from track level at Salwick on 18 April 1968 is Black 5 No. 44777 of Edge Hill Shed with 1P58, the 12.44 Preston (originally ex-London Euston) to Blackpool South. Salwick No. 2 Signal Box was opened in 1889 and closed on 10 November 2017; it was demolished soon afterwards. No. 1 Signal Box was closed in February 1973 and had been situated a short distance before the water troughs (561 yards) at Lea Lane. The troughs had been supplied with water from the adjacent Lancaster Canal and were in use from 1885 to 1967. On the right is the Springfields nuclear fuel production establishment, which began its existence as a munitions factory in 1940. At the time this picture was recorded it was still rail connected and had its own diesel shunter – a 1943 Hudswell Clarke 0-4-0DM named *Mighty Atom* (now preserved at the Ribble Steam Railway). *Below:* Virgin Trains' HST No. 43084 (with No. 43014 trailing) was photographed from the Station Road Bridge on 10 February 1999 leading a London Euston to Blackpool North Virgin Trains' InterCity train. No longer connected to the railway network, the Springfields' site is now barely visible. Lea Lane Bridge can be seen in the distance. No. 43014 later became one of the NMT Power Cars (see p. 84).

At the time this picture was recorded there were two or three trains a week from the Hillhouse ICI Plant at Burn Naze to Barry Docks for the transhipment of vinyl chloride monomer, used in the manufacture of PVC among other products. Running as 6V26, the loaded train is seen from Station Road Bridge at Salwick behind Class 47 No. 47052 (D1634) in the early evening of Sunday 21 June 1992. The wagon flow ceased to run in 1999 following closure of the works. The track bed of the widened lines is on the right.

An unidentified Pacer unit is seen in a sylvan setting approaching Kirkham & Wesham station two days after midsummer's day in 1992. The unit is working the 19.14 Colne to Blackpool South service. Dominating the scene is St Michael's Parish Church, which dates from 1822 and is a Grade II listed building.

Kirkham & Wesham station was opened on 15 July 1840. Until 2018 it only ever had two platforms, although the widened lines were laid in the late 1880s with a space to accommodate a second island platform. Platform 3 was constructed during the electrification works, which were done under a total closure of the line between 11 November 2017 and 16 April 2018. In March 2015 twenty Class 319/3 EMUs were transferred to Allerton TMD, later followed by a further fifteen. Around a dozen of these were still in use by Northern Trains in 2022. No. 319381 has stopped at platform 3 on 4 September 2022 with the 07.55 SuO Blackpool North to Liverpool Lime Street.

Blackpool has enjoyed a direct service to London for many years with the odd break now and again. The service was reintroduced by Virgin Trains on 20 May 2018 following the completion of the Fylde electrification scheme. This was later suspended due to the pandemic. Avanti West Coast recommenced the service in September 2020 using the same now rebranded Class 390 Pendolino sets with five through trains a day in each direction. No. 390001 *Bee Together* was photographed approaching a much-changed Kirkham & Wesham with the 09.48 Blackpool North to London Euston on 16 September 2022.

The Class 142 Pacer units were built at the BREL Works in Derby and first introduced in 1985; they were numbered 142001–96. Barring a couple of accident victims, the majority remained in service until November 2018 when mass withdrawals began. Unit No. 142061 (Nos 55711 and 55757) is seen on 11 June 1989 passing Fox's biscuit factory at Wesham, which had been the former Phoenix Mill, with the 15.45 Manchester Victoria to Blackpool North. Creeping up on the adjacent line is Class 47 No. 47354 (D1835) with a train of redundant concrete sleepers and bound for Kirkham tip.

DB Schenker Class 60 No. 60054 (originally named *Charles Babbage*) was photographed at the same location on 17 April 2014 at the head of UK Railtours' 'The Lancashire Hills & Coast' railtour, which had originated from London Euston at 07.25. No. 60054 had taken over the train at Warrington and travelled via Manchester, Stalybridge, Huddersfield, Hebden Bridge, Blackburn and Preston before reaching Kirkham.

At one time Kirkham North Junction Signal Box would have been extremely busy with the direct Marton line and the line to Lytham and Blackpool South both diverging at this point. The box was opened in 1903 and had 108 levers; it was closed on 10 November 2017 and demolished soon afterwards. *Above:* Class 47 No. 47588 (D1733) with DVT No. 82117 on the rear is seen passing the box on 18 March 1990 with the 09.24 Blackpool North to London Euston. The loco was painted blue in 1964 and matched up with the XP64 experimental coaching stock. Construction works for a new bridge over the line for the Kirkham bypass are in the early stages of progression. *Below:* The signal box is seen from the opposite direction with Class 104 DMU Nos 78851 and 78601 leading a Class 108 and another Class 104 with a train bound for Blackpool North on 29 June 1985. The unit had been renumbered into the experimental series following conversion to a single engine. The line to Blackpool South diverges to the right. The chimney (demolished *c.* 1987) belonged to the erstwhile Phoenix Mill, which dated from 1856.

The sight of a Merchant Navy Pacific heading for Blackpool was a rare occasion even during the preservation era. No. 35005 *Canadian Pacific* is seen near Great Plumpton at the head of Vintage Trains' 'Blackpool Belle' railtour from Nuneaton on 16 October 1999; the train had also run the week before. During the 1948 locomotive exchange trials No. 35017 *Belgian Marine* worked the northbound 'Royal Scot' from London Euston to Glasgow Central on 13 May, returning the following day with the UP train.

The direct line to Blackpool South and Central via Marton diverged from the Poulton/Fleetwood line just west of Kirkham; it was closed in 1965. However, a short spur remained for many years and was used by BR engineers as a spoil tip. Class 47 No. 47318 (D1700) has deposited a rake of four-wheeled mineral wagons and is waiting to set off back towards Kirkham and Preston. It will follow Class 150 DMU No. 150134, which has formed the 11.10 Blackpool North to Liverpool Lime Street on 28 June 1991.

A somewhat desolate scene greets the passengers at St Annes-on-Sea station on 26 October 1985 as they disembark from the 14.53 Kirkham to Blackpool South. The station was in the early stages of reconstruction, which would see a new Sainsburys store incorporated into the new design. So much for health-and-safety protocol.

A classic view from the road bridge at Poulton-le-Fylde station with the road pulled-off for Class 31 No. 31438 (D5557) with the 09.44 SuO Crewe to Blackpool North on 31 May 1992. This train was routed via Alderley Edge, Manchester Piccadilly and Salford Crescent. The semaphore signals were removed in the latter part of 2017 as part of the resignalling and electrification scheme. The Brush Type 2 was withdrawn in 1995 and is now preserved.

The line to the right was opened by the Preston & Wyre Joint Railway to Fleetwood on 15 July 1840. The passenger service was withdrawn on 1 June 1970, although freight continued to use the line as far as Burn Naze until 1999. The line to the left was laid as a branch to Blackpool North and opened on 29 April 1846. Large logo Class 47 No. 47592 (D1766) *County of Avon* is seen passing Poulton No. 3 Signal Box on 31 May 1992 with the 11.15 ECS working from Blackpool to Lancaster. The box was closed on 10 November 2017 prior to the resignalling and electrification works.

The Class 86/2s supplemented the Class 87s and 90s on the WCML until the Pendolinos came on stream in the early 2000s. No. 86249 (E3161) *County of Merseyside* has stopped at the north end of Platform 4 on 26 March 1985 with the 08.47 London Euston to Glasgow and Edinburgh, which would have divided at Carstairs.

The first Class 90s started to appear at Preston in April 1988 with the last of the fifty-strong class entering service in November 1990. Still looking pristine, No. 90002 was photographed from the footbridge leading to platforms 1 and 2 on 4 February 1989 with a London Euston to Glasgow Central train, due off Preston at 11.03.

Class 91s didn't work regular trains through Preston and No. 91001 *Swallow* was observed in platform 3 on 28 June 1993 with a return London Euston to Carlisle special working entitled the '225 Experience'. Having since been renumbered to 91101, this engine was still in operation in 2024. Examples of all the classes of main line electrics have been noted at Preston including No. 89001 *Avocet*, which worked a test train on 28 September 1987.

During the 1990s a number of cross-country services through Preston were worked by the iconic InterCity 125 Class 43 HSTs (the sets were originally numbered in the DMU series as Classes 253 and 254). Introduced in 1976, they were originally employed mainly on the ECML and the WR. However, both Plymouth Laira and Edinburgh Craigentinny TMDs later maintained a number of sets for long-distance cross-country trains. *Above:* No. 43163 was the trailing car of the 07.25 Plymouth to Aberdeen on 4 June 1993 and is seen at platform 3 with a couple of newspaper trolleys in attendance. *Below:* Again featuring the trailing power car, No. 43098 is at the rear of the departing Edinburgh Waverley to Penzance service on 7 February 1996. In later years they would be used by Virgin Trains (VT) on London to Blackpool trains. They eventually succumbed to VT's Voyager DMUs. Above the power car is in what used to be the Park Hotel, which was opened in 1882 and closed as such in 1950; the remains of the connecting station bridge (see p. 90) were not removed until *c*. 1972.

Summer Saturday trains to holiday destinations were a feature of the railways for several decades after the war. They generally faded away from the regional timetables in the late 1980s. Not surprisingly, Preston saw its fair share with a number of such trains heading for Blackpool. On 18 July 1981 Class 45 No. 45016 (D16) was photographed approaching the station with 1M89, the 08.12 SO Sheffield Midland to Blackpool North. The return working left Blackpool at 13.53 under headcode 1E57.

Virgin Trains commenced operation of the WCML franchise from 9 March 1997 and initially continued to use the existing InterCity fleet of Class 86/2, 87 and 90 electric locos. Class 87 No. 87027 *Wolf of Badenoch* is seen arriving at platform 3 with a London Euston to Glasgow Central service on 7 June 2002. The loco was withdrawn and scrapped just a few years later.

Another view taken from the same vantage point as the previous picture: the end of platform 4 (2) sees Britannia No. 70013 *Oliver Cromwell* arriving with G. C. Enterprises' 'N W Circular Tour' 1T85 from Stockport Edgeley on 28 April 1968. The Brit was in charge throughout and visited parts of both West and East Lancashire. There are seven signal gantries visible in this picture, which were all swept away a few years later under the major resignalling/remodelling programme that took place in 1971–73.

Preserved Coronation Class Pacific No. (4)6233 *Duchess of Sutherland* is seen replicating what would have been a common sight during the 1950s and early 1960s. The occasion was the Royal Touring Company's London Euston to Carlisle and return special on 10 October 2009. The semi hauled the train from/to Crewe. A comparison of the above two pictures reveals that the platform face has been moved further out.

Class 50 No. 431 (50031) draws into platform 3 on 11 September 1973 with 1S75, the 13.50 London Euston to Glasgow Central; one of fifty of the type built at Vulcan Foundry. No. 431 entered service on 1 July 1968; after eight years' service on the LMR it was transferred to Plymouth Laira TMD in May 1976 and spent another fifteen years on the WR. Now preserved at the Severn Valley Railway, it was painted into InterCity livery in 2016. (KDH Archive)

After the Class 90s had been ousted from the InterCity fleet they found gainful employment with a variety of operators on the privatised railway. Later operating for EWS, No. 90034 looks quite pristine as it heads a northbound liner train through platform 3 on 24 September 2002. This loco has also worked for Virgin Trains and Greater Anglia and was owned by DB Cargo in 2022 and stored out of service at Crewe Electric TMD.

Like some of the other locomotives featured in this book a GWR/BR Collett-designed Castle would never have ventured this far north in normal service. The last instance recalled by the author of seeing one at Preston is of the then preserved No. 7029 *Clun Castle* on a railtour on 14 October 1967. Seen in more recent times, on 20 June 2009, passing through platform 3 is No. 5043 *Earl of Mount Edgcumbe* with the 'Castle over Shap' railtour from Tyseley to Carlisle. The last Castle was turned out of Swindon Works in August 1950.

DRS Class 66 No. 66429 is seen heading north through a somewhat deserted station with 4S44, the 11.14 Daventry to Coatbridge container train on 26 July 2010. Between 2002 and 2022 DRS operated thirty-nine class 66s but not all at the same time; there were fifteen active members of the type in the fleet in 2024, of which No. 66429 was one of them.

Another class of engine that would have been unheard of at Preston in the BR era was the GWR Hall and yet on 18 May 2002 the preserved duo of No. 4965 *Rood Ashton Hall* and No. 4936 *Kinlet Hall* made for a splendid sight at the head of Vintage Trains' 1Z48, the 06.31 Birmingham New Street to Carlisle railtour. The 4-6-0 Hall Class was again designed by Collett and built at Swindon Works between 1928 and 1943 – oh, for a weed-killer train.

A celebrated appearance of an A4 at Preston was that of No. 60022 *Mallard* on 30 September 1961 with a special from Retford to Blackpool. A few years later, on 1 April 1967, the then preserved No. 4498 *Sir Nigel Gresley* passed through at the head of an A4 Locomotive Society Ltd railtour from Crewe to Carlisle. Now retired from active work, No. 60009 *Union of South Africa* stands at Preston with Pathfinder Tours' 1Z50, 'The Shap Streaker' from Birmingham New Street to Carlisle on 23 November 2002.

Above: Following the award of the WCML franchise to Richard Branson's Virgin Trains Company in March 1997, the rolling stock was revolutionised over a period of time. Introduced in 2002, the Class 221 'Tilting' Voyagers were effectively a 'Super DMU' and were generally employed on long-distance cross-country trains and the Euston to Holyhead service. No. 221112 *Ferdinand Magellan* is seen in platform 5 on 15 March 2008. *Below:* The Class 390 Pendolinos also entered service in 2002 and initially numbered fifty-three nine-coach sets; thirty-one sets later had two additional coaches inserted and four more eleven-coach sets were built in 2010–12. These were reclassified as 390/1s. Set No. 390033 was written off after an accident at Grayrigg in February 2007. Set Nos 390053 *Mission Accomplished* and 390044 *Virgin Lionheart* were occupying platforms 5 and 6 on 5 November 2008. All fifty-six sets and eighteen of the Voyagers passed to Avanti West Coast in December 2019.

The Lancaster Canal used to end just to the right of the above picture and Dock Street Coal Sidings also diverged to the right but then split at right angles with seven sidings finishing end-on to Corporation Street and a further seven running parallel to the canal as far as Marsh Lane. The canal was truncated (by 0.75 miles) at Aqueduct Street in 1964 and a few years later BR's Ladywell House was built on land which was situated on the east side of the defunct canal basin (which was then incorporated into a parking area for the building). With the closure of the Corporation Street Sidings (now occupied by retail outlets) the remainder became known as Ladywell Sidings. To facilitate the extension of Ring Way, Ladywell House was altered (partially rebuilt as the UCLAN building Brunel Court) and a new layout of engineers' sidings was laid closer to the main line. Class 20s Nos 20130 (D8130) and 20143 (D8143) were drawing a train out of the old sidings on 18 March 1990, while Class 47 No. 47819 (D1727) passes the new sidings with the 06.27 Blackpool North to London Euston on 19 May 1992.

At least one of the LNER Pacific Classes A1 to A4 passed through Preston in the 1960s while still in British Railways ownership. The power of A2 No. 60528 *Tudor Minstrel* is seen close up as it waits to depart at the north end on 23 April 1966 with the Altrincham Railway Excursion Society 1X50 'Waverley Special', which it hauled from Manchester Exchange (it paid a visit to Newton Heath shed before the tour) to Edinburgh Waverley. It was allocated to Dundee Tay Bridge MPD (62B) at the time and withdrawn six weeks later.

The forty Class AL5s (later Class 85) were built at Doncaster and entered service over the years 1961–64. They were a common sight at Preston for more than fifteen years. No. 85026 (E3081) is about to take the WCML at Maudland Junction on 1 August 1981 with the 09.33 SO Paignton to Glasgow Central. The loco was withdrawn in May 1990.

Also seen in the shadow of St Walburge's Church at Maudland Junction is Stanier Black 5 No. 44971 (10D), working hard with Target 78 from Farington Sidings to Garstang (closed to goods traffic in December 1968) on 18 April 1968. The building on the left was the old nineteenth-century Maudland's Goods Shed, which has long since disappeared. The site is now occupied by UCLAN buildings. Also just out of sight opposite the loco used to stand a water tank, which was supplied from the nearby Lancaster Canal, with water being pumped across to Preston Shed and onwards to the station and beyond.

Despite extensive testing the APT project of tilting trains on the WCML was eventually abandoned. Six prototype Class 370 APTs were trialled between 1980 and 1986, usually operating in pairs and as additional services to the timetabled trains. An unidentified set is seen heading northbound across Aqueduct Street Bridge at Tulketh on 29 August 1984. Many years later the pub in the foreground (the Lime Kiln) became a Chinese restaurant but the building was demolished in 2022. The photographer's viewpoint is the truncated end of the Lancaster Canal.

In 2013 First TransPennine Express obtained ten Siemens-built Class 350/4 EMUs to work services between Manchester Airport and Edinburgh/Glasgow. Working out of the Manchester Ardwick Depot, they replaced the Class 185 DMUs. Now sporting the First livery, No. 350404 is seen heading south at Cadley Causeway on 27 March 2017 with a train from Edinburgh Waverley to Manchester Airport. These units were in turn replaced by twelve new Class 397 Civity EMUs in November 2019. A track panel train is standing in Oxheys loop.

Among the regular Saturday afternoon freight trains in 1968 was 7P41, the Northwich (Widnes) to Whitehaven Covhops (covered hoppers dating from the 1950s), which conveyed phosphorus for the manufacture of detergents (Albright and Wilson). The last steam-hauled train was worked by Speke Junction Shed's 2-10-0 9F No. 92218 (with headboard) on 2 March 1968 and was photographed a little further north of Preston between Boys Lane and Lightfoot Lane. Three weeks later the train was noted behind Class 25 No. D5208. The slow lines were taken out of use the following year.

Just north of Lightfoot Lane DRS (Direct Rail Services) Class 88 Electro-Diesel No. 88010 *Aurora* is seen drifting south on 3 September 2022 with 4M27, the 05.48 SO Glasgow Mossend Down Yard to the Daventry International Rail Freight Terminal (DIRFT). This was one of the Carlisle/Crewe-based operator's ten Class 88s, which were built by Stadler Rail at their Valencia factory in Spain and entered service in 2017.

The Class 87s were a common sight for many years on the Anglo-Scottish expresses on the WCML. No. 87020 *North Briton* is seen speeding north at Brock (previously the site of the 560-yard-long water troughs which were replenished from the nearby Lancaster Canal) on 22 July 1991 with the 07.35 London Euston to Inverness 'Clansman'. The first three vans were for conveying motor vehicles. Completed at Crewe Works in March 1974, No. 87020 was withdrawn in December 2003.

Regular oil trains, which ran between the Stanlow Oil Refinery and either the Dalston or Jarrow Distribution Centres, were a common sight on the WCML in the 1980s and 1990s. Class 47 No. 47125 (D1715) *Tonnidae* was photographed in charge of a train of 100T bogie wagon empties returning to Stanlow at Badger Bridge (Brock) on 4 July 1989. All the trees on the right have since been felled and the adjacent M6 motorway is now in clear sight.

Sheildmuir Royal Mail Scottish Distribution Centre was opened on 8 October 1998 with trains running on a daily basis between Glasgow, Warrington and Willesden Postal Centres. The four-car Class 325 purpose-built EMUs were built at Derby in 1995–96 and initially comprised sixteen sets. With set No. 325012 leading, a train from Sheildmuir to Willesden in seen at Badger Bridge on 10 February 1999. Royal Mail announced that they would cease transferring mail by rail from mid-October 2024.

Another regular flow of freight in the same period was the transfer of steel. Class 37s Nos 37077 (D6777) and 37519 (D6727) were captured at Forton (Cleverley Bank Lane) on 20 April 1991 with a train of steel ingots, which were en route from Mossend Yard to Llanwern Steelworks where the slabs would be rolled into coil steel for various manufacturing industries.

Seen at the same location on 20 June 1992 is the 07.10 Edinburgh Waverley to Poole InterCity Cross-Country service with Class 43 power car No. 43119 (later renumbered to 43319) leading. A number of HST sets were made spare from the East Coast in 1991 with the introduction of the Class 91s and were put to work on a variety of long-distance cross-border diagrams. Having subsequently worked for GNER and EMR, the power car was in storage in 2024.

Twenty-three Class 144 DMU sets were built for the West Yorkshire Metro Network at the BREL Works in Derby in 1986–87 with collaboration on the project from Walter Alexander's, the coach and bus builder. Unit No. 144022 was photographed at Forton with an ECS working from Preston to Lancaster. These units were not a common sight in the North West; all have now been withdrawn from service.

The village of Galgate lies 16.8 miles to the north of Preston on the Anglo-Scottish main line. With a population of a little over 2,000, it had its own station (200 yards off to the left) between June 1840 and May 1939. An unidentified Class 86/2 heads south with a lengthy mail train on 8 June 1991. New houses have since been built in the foreground.

The line from Deepdale to Longridge was opened by the P&LR on 1 May 1840. Its primary objective was to convey granite stone from a number of quarries to the immediate east of Longridge. Long after this traffic ceased Courtaulds opened a factory at Ribbleton (1939) for the manufacture of Rayon, which was rail served. On 22 May 1975 Class 25 No. 25186 (D7536) was seen at Deepdale with Target 63 from Courtaulds to Farington Sidings. The trip freight ceased in early 1980 following closure of the factory.

Following the demise of steam, a variety of diesel types worked over the Longridge branch until closure in 1994; these included Classes 20, 25, 31, 40, 47 and 56s. On 9 May 1980 Class 40 No. 40106 (D306) had taken an engineer's train along the single line and was photographed at Deepdale on the return journey. At the time, No. 40106 was something of a celebrity loco and was painted green with the BR lion and wheel emblem.

Class 20s working the Deepdale coal train were fairly uncommon. However, on 16 May 1986 Wigan TMD-based Nos 20042 (D8042) and 20209 (D8309) were seen on the coal depot sidings line connecting up to the empties. The three cement wagons had actually discharged their load at Maudland at the start of the branch. This line also led to the original Deepdale Street station (1840–56). (Martyn Hilbert)

The branch was originally built as double track as far as Skeffington Road – it was reduced to single in around the early 1970s. Following the closure of the Lancashire collieries the coal was subsequently transported a much greater distance and latterly came from Barry Docks in South Wales. Class 37 No. 37223 (D6923) was photographed with the empties between Deepdale Road and St Paul's Road on 22 August 1991.

Another unusual loco on the branch was Class 47 No. 47145 (D1738) *MERDDIN EMRYS*, which is seen on route learning/inspection duties on 29 August 1991. This section of line through to Maudland was opened on 1 November 1856. Deepdale Road Bridge is in the distance and the two-platform station, officially closed on 2 June 1930, was situated just before the bridge. 'DEEPDALE STATION' was a destination on the Corporation's trams.

While the main Longridge line passed under Deepdale Mill Street the close-by branch to the coal depot crossed it on the level. Class 37 No. 37796 was in the process of drawing out the empty HEA wagons when photographed on the crossing on 31 March 1994. In 2024 the tracks still remained in the road surface but the permanent way was fenced off. New buildings now occupy the empty plots of land.

To see one loco on the Longridge branch was an occasion but to see two at the same time was almost unheard of. Class 37 No. 37895 (D6819) and Class 31 No. 31134 (D5552) were photographed from Skeffington Road on 12 May 1994. The 37 has drawn the rake of HEAs out of the coal depot and then crossed over the road with the 31 backing on to take the consist back towards Preston. The reason for this unusual manoeuvre remains a mystery.

Class 31 No. 31134 (D5552) is seen approaching Maudland Curve Junction with the rescued train. It is doubtful that the Type 2 would have taken the train all the way back to South Wales. On the right is the site of Maudland Bridge station (which had a brief existence from 1856–85). Access to the platform was from Cold Bath Street under which the rear of the train is passing. The Lancaster Canal used to pass under the bridge in the centre of the picture.

Platforms 10, 11 and 12 were all bay platforms on the East Lancs side. On 10 February 1968 Black 5 No. 44971 (10D) is seen departing platform 10 with 3P26, the 10.40 Preston to Colne Parcels. No. 44971 was built at Crewe in April 1946 and lasted in service until the end of steam.

3P26 is seen again on 4 May 1968. Black 5 No. 45407 (10D) on this occasion is waiting for the off on platform 13. This was a through platform and was the last to be added as such to the station complex in 1913, having previously been another bay platform. Note the Fish Dock Area in the background. Normally based at the East Lancashire Preservation Railway, the loco was part of the stable for the 'Jacobite' programme of trains in 2022.

Stanier 8F No. 48253 (10D) was photographed at the south end of platform 13 on 17 February 1968 in charge of 7P78, the 08.35 Wyre Dock to Rose Grove empty coal train. No. 48253 was built at the North British Works in Glasgow in July 1941 and was another loco which lasted until the end of steam. The brick building was one of two separate goods sheds built by the ELR in the adjacent yard. Closed in around early 1973, the two goods sheds weren't demolished until the mid-1980s to facilitate the building of the Fishergate Shopping Centre.

Seen in exactly the same location on 5 August 1972 is English Electric Type 4, later designated Class 40, No. 278. It is in charge of 1S44, the 10.02 SO Blackpool North to Glasgow Central, and would work round the loop via Todd Lane and Farington and then travel back north through the station. The whole of the East Lancs side of the station was taken out of use before the end of the year. Bay platforms 11 and 12 are on the left. (KDH Archive)

Stanier 8F No. 48062 (10F) is seen standing at the north end of platform 8 (later renumbered to 6) on 26 February 1968 leaking steam everywhere and waiting for the road with 6P32, the 13.10 Rose Grove to Wyre Dock loaded coal train. The adjacent tracks are splitting to run through platforms 9 and 13. Butler Street is above the adjacent wall.

Black 5 No. 45350 (10F) is seen departing Preston on the East Lancs line on 23 April 1968 and is about to cross the river bridge. It is in charge of 7N79, the 10.45 Wyre Dock to Healey Mills Marshalling Yard; the latter opened in 1963. Just visible above the last wagon is Preston E L Signal Box, which replaced an earlier box in 1873 and was closed in February 1973.

Empty coal working 7N79 is seen again the following day with Rose Grove's Black 5 No. 45382 in charge, which is climbing the gradient at Hospital Foot Crossing, a short distance to the east of Bamber Bridge. Even in the last months of steam the East Lancashire line was still very busy with steam-hauled freights. The 4-6-0 was withdrawn on 29 June 1968.

Further east towards Blackburn and Class 60 No. 60070 *John Loudon McAdam* was captured on film at Gregson Lane on 1 May 1992 with the SO Padiham Power Station to Workington empty coal-box wagons. Built at the Brush Works in Loughborough in October 1991, the loco, now owned by DC Rail, was back there in store some thirty years later.

Large logo Class 47 No. 47436 (D1552) is seen passing through Blackburn with the diverted 09.09 Glasgow Central to Brighton on 11 March 1989. The loco was turned out from Crewe Works in January 1964 and was withdrawn in December 1991. It was cut up at MC Metals in Glasgow in August 1993.

The line from Blackburn to Bolton was built by the Blackburn, Darwen & Bolton Railway (BD&BR) and was eventually opened throughout on 12 June 1848. At one time double track, this 14-mile section was substantially reduced to a single line in 1973. Entwistle is now the second stop on the route after Darwen and Pacer unit Class 142 DMU No. 142058 (Nos 55708 and 55754) is seen approaching the single platform on 22 July 1991 with the 16.05 Blackburn to Rochdale. A lone passenger waits to board the train. The service was extended from/ to Clitheroe in May 1994. The unit is now preserved at the Telford Steam Railway.

Preserved rebuilt Bullied West Country (WC) Pacific No. 34027 (SR 21C127) *Taw Valley* was in charge of Flying Scotsman Services' 1C99 'Cumbrian Mountain Express' on 14 December 1991. The train had left London Euston behind an AC Electric at 08.20 with the WC coming on at Lostock Hall Junction for the journey to Carlisle via the S&C. The train is seen at Wilpshire on the outskirts of Blackburn.

A few weeks earlier, on 14 September 1991, preserved LNER Gresley 2-6-2 V2 No. 4771 (60800) *Green Arrow* was photographed at the same location with Hertfordshire Rail Tours' 'The Border City Limited'. This was a dining special from the Midlands to Carlisle. The engine was on loan from the NRM and on static display in a Doncaster museum in 2024. A total of 184 V2s were built at York and Darlington between 1936 and 1944.

On 17 May 1980 this unusual combination was photographed with the SLOA 'Lancastrian' railtour 1L06, the 14.16 Carnforth to Manchester Victoria via Settle Junction. Running two hours late, it was hauled by Class 47 No. 47522 (D1105) and preserved Midland Compound No. 1000. The Johnson 4F 4-4-0 was built at Derby in 1902 and was being conveyed to Rainhill for the Rocket 150 celebrations.

Among other phenomena, Whalley is famous for its magnificent viaduct comprising forty-eight arches and built out of red and blue bricks between 1846 and 1850. Riddles Standard 4-6-2 No. 71000 *Duke of Gloucester* drifts across the bridge on 1 June 1991 with Flying Scotsman Services Ltd's 1A99, the 15.04 Appleby to London Euston 'Cumbrian Mountain Express'.

GBRF Class 66 No. 66740 *Sarah* is seen passing Clitheroe Interchange with 6M90, the 05.06 Avonmouth Hanson Sidings to Clitheroe Castle Cement on 24 June 2020. The train is within a mile of its final destination. At the time bus services in the area were being provided by Preston Bus, and Pilkington Bus, represented here by Optare Solo SRs No. 20708 (PN08 SVU) and No. 2 (YJ64 DSE) from the respective fleets.

The Ribblesdale Cement Company at Clitheroe was founded in 1937. Following a number of mergers and name changes, it was trading as Hanson Cement (Heidelberg Cement Group) in 2024. Former BR Type 1 Class 17 D8568 became the only one of its type to survive. It was first sold by BR in 1972 and acquired by Ribble Cement in June 1977 and remained there until early 1983 when it was sold for preservation. It was photographed at the cement plant on 3 May 1982. In 2024 it was owned by the Diesel Traction Group and based at the Chinnor & Princes Risborough Railway. (Martyn Hilbert)

Following the purchase of A3 4-6-2 No. 60103 (LNER No. 4472) *Flying Scotsman* by Alan Pegler in 1963 it appeared on a number of railtours in the North West in the late 1960s. One such tour was organised by the Williams Deacon's Bank Club and ran on 17 March 1968 and involved two separate trains which required the use of seven steam locomotives comprising A3 No. 4472, Britannia No. 70013 *Oliver Cromwell* and Black 5s Nos 44899, 45110/203/90/447. Train No. 1 ran as 1L30 and 'Scotsman' hauled the train from Stockport Edgeley to Accrington piloted by Black 5 No. 45290 (26C/9K) from Bolton. Seen among the throngs of onlookers at Accrington, No. 4472 is about to be replaced by Black 5 No. 44899 (10F) for the onward journey to Skipton where No. 4472 would again take charge of the train for the next leg of the journey to Carnforth. No. 45447 is waiting for the second train.

The inauguration of a new service from Blackpool/Preston to Leeds/York in 1984 was influenced by the opening of a new office complex by the Halifax Building Society in Halifax some ten years previously. The building society had lobbied for a direct service from Lancashire to the Yorkshire town for the benefit of its employees. Metro-liveried Class 155 Sprinter No. 155342 was photographed coming off the nineteen-arch stone viaduct in the centre of Accrington on 10 October 1992 with the 09.18 Leeds to Blackpool North. The viaduct was built by the original ELR in 1847.

Also seen on a Calder Valley working at a much simplified Accrington station on 16 March 1991 is Class 156 No. 156473 with the 08.15 from Leeds to Blackpool North. The two-car 158 sets later gave way to a dedicated batch of three-car sets, which in turn were replaced by new Class 195 DMUs. At one time Accrington boasted a triangular junction with four platforms, a goods shed, a carriage shed, a locomotive depot (coded 24A and later 10E) and extensive sidings.

Sunday 4 August 1968 is a date which is etched in the memory of all rail enthusiasts of a certain age as it was the last day that BR steam worked on the network. No less than five steam-hauled specials were booked to pass through Blackburn. *Above:* The LCGB 1Z74 'Farewell to Steam Rail Tour' arrived at Blackburn from Manchester Victoria behind Britannia No. 70013 *Oliver Cromwell* (10A) piloting Black 5 No. 44781 (10A). Here the Brit was replaced by 8F No. 48773 (10F), which is seen backing on to the train at the east end of the station for the onward journey to Carnforth. *Below:* The SLS ran two specials which followed the same itineraries. The second of the two ran as 1Z79 the 'Farewell to Steam No. 2'. The train had originated at Birmingham New Street and was hauled by Black 5s Nos 44874 (10A) and 45017 (10A) from Manchester Victoria to Stockport via Huddersfield, Copy Pit, Blackburn, Wigan, Rainhill and Manchester Victoria. The train is seen at the west end of the station.

There has been a regular flow of cement from Clitheroe to the Hanson Sidings at Avonmouth for a number of years. On 9 August 2018 GBRF Class 66 No. 66766 is seen leading No. 66768 through Bamber Bridge with 6V82; the latter locomotive had previously failed. Not long after this picture was recorded a flying buttress support was placed between the signal box and the opposite building to give the box some stability.

Bamber Bridge station has had a basic hourly service in each direction for many years and was served by the Preston to Colne stopping train. Trains to and from York/Leeds also pass through but don't stop here. Northern Rail Merseyrail-liveried Pacer unit Class 142 No. 142052 pauses at the eastbound platform on 11 March 2006 with a train for Colne. Bamber Bridge is well known among the local football supporters' fraternity for its processional coffin ritual/burial (based on the 1960s TV programme *All Gas and Gaiters*), which traditionally takes place following a relegation season by either Preston North End or Blackburn Rovers. The coffin is exhumed if one of the teams gains promotion.

Locomotive Services Ltd, which was based at Crewe, acquired a number of HST power cars and painted them in a pseudo-Midland Pullman livery of blue and white, thereby replicating the original train of the 1960s. On 22 June 2024 No. 43055 (with No. 43059 leading) was on the rear of special train 1Z44, the 06.47 from Holyhead to Carlisle via the Settle & Carlisle Line as it passed through Bamber Bridge. Note the flying buttress support for the signal cabin.

At one time Castle Cement (later Hanson) at Clitheroe provided a regular flow to Gunnie (Coatbridge) in Scotland. It was usually worked by a pair of Type 3s and is seen at Lostock Hall Junction on 2 June 1992 headed by Class 37s Nos 37676 (D6826) and 37677 (D6821). The line to the left used to lead round to Todd Lane, while the line by the lighting pylon was the third side of the triangle with Bamber Bridge Engineering Sidings adjacent to it. The rail connection on the right leads into W. H. Bowker's Distribution Depot and was only constructed in July 1990; the connection remains but is no longer used.

Preserved English Electric Type 4 No. D213 (40013) *Andania* and Type 5 Class 50 No. 50050 (D400) *Fearless* are seen at the head of 1Z62, the 15.04 Preston to Hellifield special train passing Lostock Hall Junction on 10 August 2024. It is hard to believe there used to be sidings both on the right and between the two lines and the new Lostock Hall station, opened on 14 May 1984, can just be seen before the overbridge (having previously been on the other side of the bridge). The line to the left was the ELR's original connection to the NUR which opened in 1846 and curved north (it now joins the main line in a southerly direction) at Farington to join the NUR just south of Farington station.

Lostock Hall Shed was opened by the LYR with due ceremony on 3 June 1882 and latterly consisted of eight partly covered roads with capacity for around forty locos. On 30 April 1966 Royston Shed's WD 2-8-0 No. 90338 (WD70814) was taking a breather. 10D (24C prior to 1963) had its own allocation of WDs, which among other duties were gainfully employed on trip freights and the coal trains from Yorkshire to Burn Naze and Wyre Dock. The last of the type were withdrawn by BR in September 1967.

Referred to by many local enthusiasts as 'City of Preston', Jinty Fowler 3F 0-6-0T No. 47472 (LMS No. 16555) began its Lancashire career at Preston Shed in September 1952 before transferring to 10D in September 1961. It was withdrawn w/e 26 November 1966. Nos 47314 (also withdrawn) and 47472 were photographed on 1 January 1967. It had been a frequent performer on station pilot duties throughout its fourteen years in the area.

The Ivatt 2-6-0 was a late arrival to the locality, although over the last few years of steam operation at least eleven different examples spent time at 10D. Built at Horwich in February 1949, No. 43027 was transferred from Workington Shed in January 1968. It was withdrawn in May and cut up at Arnott Young's yard in Dinsdale in the North East five months later. It was photographed on 4 May 1968 at the head of the breakdown train on No. 1 road. Behind the loco was the original Lostock Hall station, which was closed on 6 October 1969.

Horwich-built Stanier Black 5 4-6-0 No. 44950 is turned on the 70-foot turntable at Lostock Hall on Saturday 3 August 1968. It had only been transferred to 10D from Speke Junction (8C) in April. It was not involved with the following day's special trains.

Riddles Britannia 4-6-2 No. 70013 *Oliver Cromwell* stands under the 90,000-gallon-capacity water tank at Lostock Hall Shed on 3 August 1968. Adjacent to the tank was a water softening plant. The tank received water from the Lancaster Canal, which was first collected in a pump house at Fylde Road (under one of the bridge arches) and was then pumped into a tank at the trackside and through a pipe system to another tank at Pedder Street and then onward to an auxiliary pump house at Vicars Bridge. Finally it was piped adjacent to the ELR towards Todd Lane and then onwards to the shed (a distance of 3.7 miles[1]). Water was also taken from nearby Farington Lodge. The shed closed to locomotive servicing in 1971 but continued to be used to maintain other rolling stock for a number of years.

Somewhat of a celebrity locomotive, preserved Class 25 No. D7672 (25322/912) *Tamworth Castle* is seen passing the site of Lostock Hall Shed (on the left) and the original station while hauling Hertfordshire Rail Tours 'Copy Pit Pullman' from London Euston on 29 December 1990. The Type 2 worked the train from Preston to Leeds where Class 91 No. 91013 *County of North Yorkshire* took over for the run back to London King's Cross. The shed site had only been cleared in January of that year and the site still remained derelict in 2024 while the caravan dealership was still trading. (Martyn Hilbert)

Speke Junction's 2-10-0 9F No. 92054 had been borrowed to work 7N87, the 10.50 North Union Sidings to Royston (Cudworth) Sidings empty coal train on 19 April 1968. It was photographed climbing the 1 in 78 gradient of Farington Curve; the curve was opened in 1908 and connected the Lostock Hall/Ormskirk line to the LNWR (NUR) main line. The 9F was withdrawn just sixteen days later. This location is now totally treed-in with new houses having been built on the land to the right. Coote Lane bridge is in the background.

Climbing Farington Curve some thirty-one years later was preserved Class 55 English Electric Deltic D9000 (55022) *Royal Scots Grey* while on loan to Virgin Trains. It was working a diverted Birmingham International to Edinburgh Waverley service on 13 March 1999, which was routed via the S&C to Carlisle. (Martyn Hilbert)

Both the Ormskirk (1891) and the East Lancashire (1908) lines join the WCML at Farington Curve Junction, although they were not connected at the same time. The 09.45 Colne to Preston was photographed on 27 April 1984 with Newton Heath DMU sets Class 108 car Nos 53930 and 51563 leading and Class 104 car Nos 53425 and 53439 trailing about to join the main line. These first-generation DMUs would later be replaced by Pacers.

InterCity Class 47 No. 47841 (D1726) *The Institution of Mechanical Engineers* is seen joining the WCML at Farington Curve Junction on 3 August 1991 with 1V39, the 07.35 Summer SO Rose Grove to Paignton; this train ran for a number of years with differing departure times. The Type 4 was turned out of the Brush Works at Loughborough in March 1964 and was first allocated to Cardiff Canton TMD. It was owned by Locomotive Services Ltd (LSL) in 2024, having been used as a source of spares.

One of the last regular steam-hauled passenger trains out of Preston in 1968 was 1F46, the 16.40 Preston to Liverpool Exchange. This train originated at Glasgow and divided at Preston, with the remaining portion proceeding to Manchester Victoria. Black 5 No. 45212 (10D) was photographed climbing Farington Moss Curve on 14 April 1968. The curve was built in 1891 to connect the Ormskirk to Lostock Hall line to the LNWR main line at Farington. The 4-6-0 is now preserved at the Worth Valley Railway.

After the direct trains to Liverpool via Ormskirk ceased to run in May 1970 and the truncated service became solely worked by DMUs, the presence of a locomotive on the line became something of a rarity. However, on 22 May 1993 Class 56 No. 56027 was photographed at Croston with 1Z46, the Preston to Ormskirk leg of Pathfinders Tours' 'Lancastrian Mini-Excursions'. Class 37 No. 37706 was on the rear of the train.

Following the cessation of through trains to Liverpool the line was singled as far as Ormskirk with a single passing loop at Rufford. Class 104 DMU Nos 50474 and 50556 call at the now single-platform Croston station with a train for Ormskirk on 22 April 1982. Car No. 50474 was scrapped at Vic Berry's Leicester yard in April 1989, while No. 50556, which had been first allocated to South Gosforth MPD in October 1958, was saved for preservation but was ultimately stripped for spares in 2020.

Newton Heath also had an allocation of Class 105 Craven's DMUs. The old units provided a bird's eye view through the driver's cab area and this has been used to good effect by the photographer to capture this scene, which features an unidentified Class 105 approaching Rufford on 14 May 1977 with the 17.56 Preston to Ormskirk. The signal box was opened in 1875 but was replaced by a portacabin with a handful of switches in 1988.

A local stopping service had been introduced to serve the three remaining intermediate stations as far as Ormskirk. The single-car Class 153 conversions were ideal units for the branch and could be seen on the service for many years. No. 153317 is seen at Ormskirk on 3 October 2012. The Northern 153s were maintained at Leeds Neville Hill and Heaton TMDs and out stationed throughout the extensive Northern operating area.

Ormskirk station lies just beyond the mid-point of what was originally the through line from Preston to Liverpool Exchange, which was opened by the LO&PR in April 1849. A line was opened by the ELR from Ormskirk to St Helens via Skelmersdale in March 1858 and in later years was operated by a steam railmotor, which acquired the name of the 'Jazzer'. After using temporary accommodation for its locomotives the LYR built a new four-road shed in 1893. The shed closed in September 1935, while the line to Skelmersdale closed to passengers on 5 November 1956. The line from Liverpool had been electrified as early as 1913 using the third rail system and operated by a variety of EMUs. The second generation of EMUs was built by the LMS at Derby and comprised 152 cars, which could operate as either two- or three-car sets. *Above:* A three-car Class 502 is seen in a somewhat run-down environment with a train for Liverpool on 16 April 1977. The 502s had been phased out by 1980 by new EMUs, Classes 507/8, which were built at York. *Below:* Seen in a now somewhat overgrown vista, unit No. 507013 also waits to depart with a train for Liverpool some thirty-three years later. These units were replaced by a fourth generation of EMUs, the class 777, in 2024.

The line down to the docks (originally Victoria Quay) was opened by the North Union Railway in 1846 and was still in use in 2024. Besides the regular bitumen train from Immingham to the Lanfina Depot (Total Bitumen) the line also saw occasional special trains visiting the Ribble Steam Railway. *Above:* Colas Class 70 No. 70817 is about to dive down the 1 in 29 gradient with 6M32 from the Lindsey Refinery on 17 April 2019. The Class 70s were operated by both Colas and Freightliner and were built by General Electric at their factory in Erie, Pennsylvania. *Below:* Apart from a break between 1995 and 2004, this train had been running since at least the late 1960s (latterly from Teesside) and on 20 June 2012 Class 60 No. 60099 was caught emerging alongside the station with the return empties, 6E32. The 100-ton TEA bogie wagons were first introduced on to the railway in 1980; these fairly new 102-ton VTG bogie wagons were built by Axiom Rail at Stoke-on-Trent in 2010. The train has been worked successively by BR, EWS, DB Schenker UK and Colas Rail. The train ceased to run in October 2024.

Following damage to an overbridge on the branch in 1995 6M32 ceased to run to the docks and was diverted to run to the depot at Ashton-in-Makerfield. After nine years' absence and a lot of behind-the-scenes negotiations and preparation the train was reinstated in 2004. Class 37 No. 37211 (D6911) leads a train across Strand Road bound for Immingham on 17 August 1976. The Type 3 was withdrawn in August 2003 and scrapped at EMR's (European Metal Recycling Ltd) yard at Kingsbury in Tamworth.

At one time the Lanfina Tar and Petrofina Oil depots each received separate train loads of tar and oil but by the 1990s these had been combined to form a single train and in 1992 the Petrofina site closed. On 31 October 1984 Class 56 No. 56101 is seen with a mixed train of tar and oil wagons. The new exchange sidings had only recently been brought into use when this picture was recorded.

On 15 July 1991 Class 31 No. 31201 (D5625) *Fina Energy* was being flagged across Strand Road with its rake of empty tar wagons. This method of stopping the traffic was used for decades until control barriers were eventually installed in the 2000s. Accidents were few and far between but on 5 September 1984 Class 56 No. 56107 collided with a Preston Borough Transport Leyland Atlantean – fortunately, the bus was empty and the bus driver was uninjured.

The Dock Authority purchased seven new 0-6-0 saddle tanks from W. G. Bagnall of Stafford between 1942 and 1948. These carried the names *Conqueror*, *Courageous*, *Energy*, *Enterprise*, *Perseverance*, *Princess* and *Progress*. During the 1950s the docks was extremely busy with some twelve trains per weekday working to and from Bamber Bridge Sidings. The last of the type was withdrawn in September 1968. *Progress* is seen at rest between duties on 1 December 1965.

A rake of wooden internal Preston Corporation user wagons is seen alongside the Victoria Warehouse on the south quayside on 31 October 1976. In the past these would have been used to convey unloaded cargo to one of the warehouses. There was also a number of PC labelled box vans; at its height there was some 28 miles of track in the dock complex. Victoria Warehouses (Shed No. 3) still stands and is now known as Victoria Mansions, having been fully refurbished as living accommodation.

Thomas W. Ward established a number of breakers yards around the country way back in the late nineteenth century. Innumerable (over 400) ships were broken up at the river quayside at Preston between 1894 and 1970. In attendance at the yard on 31 October 1976 was this 0-4-0DM *PRESIDENT*, which was built by John Fowler of Leeds in 1956.

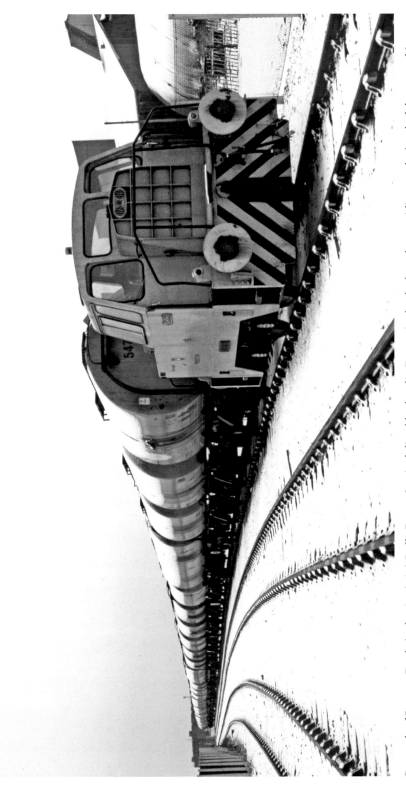

Borough of Preston Dock Authority 0-4-0 Rolls-Royce Sentinel diesel hydraulic *Energy* in the dock exchange sidings at the head of the empty bitumen tanks on 24 January 1985. *Energy* was one of three Sentinel diesels, the others being *Enterprise* and *Progress*, which replaced the Bagnall tank engines in 1968. *Energy* was later sold on, while the other two continued to work at the docks, having been joined by another Sentinel in 2004, which again took the name of *Energy*.

The year 1992 was a 'Guild' year and the Borough Council organised an event on the docks which included providing a steam-hauled service train on the fairly new rerouted Dock Branch – this was more than a decade before the Ribble Steam Railway came to Preston. At the time, former Agecroft Colliery Robert Stephenson & Co. and Hawthorn Leslie 1948-built 0-4-0ST *Agecroft No. 2* was based at the Steamport Museum in Southport but an agreement was made for the diminutive tank engine to pay a visit to Preston. This took place over the early May Day bank holiday. *Above: Agecroft No. 2* is seen outside the Dock Authority engine shed along with Class 47 No. 47278, which was also on display. *Below:* A temporary platform was constructed close to the exchange sidings and No. 2 ran a shuttle service along the branch from Strand Road to close to the Lanfina Depot. Andrew Barclay 1952 0-4-0ST No. 22, which was visiting from the Embsay & Bolton Abbey Steam Railway, was attached to the opposite end of the train to enable bi-directional running. In this vista the development at the east end of the dock and St Walburge's Church are both clearly visible – a view that is now obscured by trees. Both views were recorded on Sunday 3 May.

After years of planning the Ribble Steam Railway finally opened its doors to the travelling public in January 2004. Many of the locomotives on site had come from the erstwhile Steamport site in Southport. Much-travelled former GWR 0-6-2T No. 5643 was in charge of the two-coach passenger train on the 1.25-mile-long line on 6 February 2010. The loco was turned out of Swindon Works in 1925 and later rescued from Barry Scrapyard.

As redevelopment work at Riversway (Docklands) progressed the internal railway line was relaid alongside the north bank of the river and then across the mouth of the dock basin over a new swing bridge, which was commissioned in 1986. The line then continued to the Petrofina Oil and Lanfina Tar depots. Class 66s Nos 66103 and 66009 were photographed on the bridge on 25 June 2005 with the return Branch Line Society's 'Aire & Ribble Pioneer' railtour from the Ribble Steam Railway to Ealing Broadway.

A number of special trains have travelled the full length of the dock branch as far as the Steam Railway Complex. *Above:* On 19 January 2008 Class 67 No. 67029 *Royal Diamond* was leading UK Railtours' 'The Preston Docker' railtour 1Z66 from London Euston to Preston Docks via Bescot and Wolverhampton. The train is seen crossing the swing bridge and was tailed by Class 37 No. 37401 (D6968). The next leg of the journey took the train to Heysham Port before returning to London. *Below:* Nearly ten years later, on 15 June 2017, DRS Class 68 No. 68026 *Enterprise*, with Class 66 No. 66432 on the rear, was also seen crossing the bridge with the return journey of the Branch Line Society's 'The Cat and Dock' railtour 1Z49 to Ormskirk, Preston Dock and Liverpool Lime Street. The train had originated at Stafford and travelled via a number of unusual sections of track before arriving at the docks.

The Steam Railway Exhibition Hall is a modern building with an interesting collection of locos on view. In 2012 the Napier 'DELTIC' arrived back in the city of its manufacture and was put on extended display in the hall for over three years. It was built at the then nearby English Electric Works in 1955. It arrived and departed under its own steam, so to speak.

The sight of a 'Western' at Preston in BR days would have caused the local railway enthusiast fraternity to endure a state of conniption as diesel hydraulics didn't normally venture north of Crewe. Main line-certified No. D1015 *Western Champion* was caught on camera departing platform 5 on 4 August 2007 in charge of Pathfinders Tours' 'Cumbrian Mountain Express' from Preston to Swindon. It was making its way back to its then base at Old Oak Common having spent some time on the ELPR. Class 22 (Nos D6300–57) and 43 (Nos D832–65) hydraulics would have passed through Preston between the years 1959 and 1962 on delivery from the North British Works to the Western Region.

Many different varieties of departmental rolling stock have passed through Preston over the years. Indeed, the Dock Street Sidings has been used by Network Rail for engineering purposes for many years. *Above:* The New Measurement Train was launched in 2003 and is normally based at the Derby Research Centre. Three power cars were converted for use with the train. No. 43013 is seen at the rear of the set on 16 February 2016; Nos 43014/62 were the other two power cars which formed part of the original set-up. *Below:* The Track Recording Unit was based on the body of a two-car Class 150/1 DMU and was built in 1987. It was still in use in 2024 having covered many thousands of miles throughout the whole of the UK's rail network. In this view it has paused at platform 5 on 24 April 2008.

In July 2003 the TransPennine Express franchise was awarded to FirstGroup and Keolis as a joint venture. The Class 185 DMUs comprised fifty-one sets and were built in Krefeld in Germany; they were maintained at Manchester Ardwick TMD. Sets Nos 185102 and 185149 were bound for Barrow-in-Furness and Manchester Airport, respectively, on 7 October 2012. They were also originally used on services to Glasgow and Edinburgh before being replaced by new EMUs.

The Class 92 electric loco was built at the Brush Works in Loughborough from 1993 to 1996 and has proved to be a somewhat underused engine with a number of the type having been transferred abroad. No. 92017, in special Stobart Rail livery (operated by DB Schenker), heads north through platform 5 on 14 June 2010 with the daily weekday 4S43, the 06.31 Tesco Express from Daventry (DIRFT) to the Grangemouth Rail Terminal.

Preston station in June 2010 and four types of second-generation DMUs epitomise the type of local trains to be seen at the time. *Above*: Class 142 No. 142091 waits to depart platform 2 with a local stopping service to Ormskirk, while Class 150 No. 150141 has terminated in platform 3 with a train from Manchester. *Below*: TransPennine Express unit No. 185132 is standing in platform 4 with a train for Manchester Airport and finally Class 156 No. 156429 is waiting at platform 5 to form the next hourly service to Hazel Grove via Manchester Piccadilly. The magnificent station roof canopy was constructed of cast iron and steel with glass panels in the late 1870s as part of the extensive station reconstruction works undertaken at the time, jointly by the LNWR and the LYR; designed by Cooper & Tullis, the station is now a Grade II listed building.

From 2002 Virgin Trains received the first of an eventual sixteen Class 57 'Thunderbird' locos, which were re-engineered from redundant Class 47s. One or two of the type were usually stabled at Preston. On 6 December 2008 No. 57307 *Lady Penelope* (formerly Class 47 No. 47225) was engaged in assisting Pendolino No. 390031 *City of Liverpool* over a diversion route.

On 4 February 2010 new-build A1 Pacific No. 60163 *Tornado* was engaged on special duties when it hauled the Royal Train from Preston to the Manchester Museum of Science & Industry via Golborne Junction; on board were HRH Prince Charles and Lady Camilla. A Class 67 was attached to the opposite end. The Prince of Wales feathers are proudly displayed on the smokebox door. Note the now-completed five-storey car park in the background. It was built on the site of the former ELR engine stabling point and carriage sidings.

The Carlisle to Chirk (Kronospan) log train usually ran via the Settle & Carlisle line but on 21 May 2014 6J37 was routed direct via the WCML. Class 56 No. 56087 was one of ten of the type operated by Colas Rail at the time. No. 56087 was built at Doncaster Works in December 1980.

LMS Princess Class Pacific No. 6201 *Princess Elizabeth* was photographed waiting to take over a railtour from London to Glasgow on 16 November 2006. The following day the Princess returned as the Mid-day Scot to commemorate the seventieth anniversary of its own long-distance high-speed record-breaking run. Note the mezzanine floor covering, which was laid on top of the original mastic asphalt on platforms 3 and 4.

As previously mentioned BR conducted an extensive programme of trial runs with their futuristic APT design concept. Known as the 'Tilting Train', its ultimate downfall was in fact its tilting capabilities as two trains passing on a canted curve were deemed to pass too close to one another. Set No. 376006 is seen at platform 6 on 7 September 1984. (Ian McLoughlin)

The ninety-eight Class 33s were based on the Southern Region during their BR operating days and would not have been seen at Preston. However, three of the type were acquired by West Coast Railways in September 2005. Based at nearby Carnforth, they could be seen from time to time on coaching stock positioning moves. On 21 June 2010 No. 33207 (D6592) *Jim Martin* was on such a duty and is seen heading south through platform 4.

The two south-end bay platforms were put in during the remodelling of the station in the late 1870s. For much of their existence they were known as 5A and 6A. Following the second remodelling exercise over ninety years later they were renumbered to 3C and 4C. Over the years they have proved to be a useful asset and performed several functions. These have included stabling steam locomotives waiting to take over southbound trains, loading/unloading parcels vans, stabling diesel and electric locos and the departure point for short trains, particularly the Ormskirk service. *Above*: Black 5 No. 45305 (10D) has deposited its vans in 6A (4C) having arrived with 3P14 from Blackpool North on 17 May 1968. The remains of 'Glass Bridge' can be seen on the right. *Below:* Uniquely liveried Class 86 No. 86401 *Northampton Town* in NSE livery was stabled in 3C on 8 September 1991. The enclosed bridge in the background was constructed in the mid-1960s and housed a conveyor belt/hook system to transport mail bags from the West Cliff Sorting Office to platforms 5/6 (3/4). It has since been removed following the closure of the Sorting Office.

When the NUR was originally built there were just two tracks spanning a bridge over the Ribble. This was then increased to five and finally to seven with the addition of the goods lines in 1903. An unidentified VT HST power car is seen heading a London-bound train across the river on 13 March 1999. Visible under the right-hand arch is the 'New' Continental Hotel, complete with its own bowling green, which was established in 1911 and has been dispensing fine ales ever since (photographed from the ELR bridge).

Seen from a trackside vantage point on 16 February 1985 is Class 86 No. 86260 (E3144) *Driver Wallace Oakes GC* which has just replaced a Type 4 diesel on the 09.34 Blackpool North to London Euston. Sixty-one of the original AL6 electrics were re-classified as Class 86/2s which were fitted with upgraded bogies for high-speed running. This loco was latterly renumbered to No. 86702 and later exported to Bulgaria in 2016. Class 08 diesel shunters had taken over station pilot duties from the Jinties in the mid-1960s.

Trains were remarshalled on a regular basis in Ribble Sidings just south of the river bridge. The sidings originally consisted of three tracks but these were increased to six as part of the 1901–03 remodelling scheme; they were taken out of use in around the late 1980s. Class 25 No. 25230 (D7580) is depicted departing Ribble Sidings with a train of mineral wagons on 16 February 1985. The mass of catenary gives the scene a surreal look.

Preserved Coronation Class 4-6-2 Pacific No. 46229 *Duchess of Hamilton* is seen heading north at Skew Bridge on 3 October 1995 with the Days Out Ltd's 'Shap Time Trial' railtour from Crewe to Carlisle via the WCML. The Duchess was built at Crewe by the LMS in September 1938 and was originally streamlined; it was withdrawn on 15 February 1964. It is now a static exhibit in the National Railway Museum.

Bee Lane road bridge crossed over the main line at Farington Curve Junction. In this busy scene, recorded on 15 July 1993, Class 37s Nos 37675 (D6864) and 37416 (D6602) are seen heading the empty Irvine to Burngullow 'silver bullet' china-clay train. Pacer unit No. 142033 is on a local service to Colne and will diverge onto the ELR under the bridge. Skew Bridge is in the distance. By 2024 the houses had become totally obscured by lineside growth.

A fairly regular source of freight traffic which still passed through Preston in 2024 was the conveyance of nuclear flasks to and from Sellafield BNFL in Cumbria. On 11 April 1992 Class 31 No. 31200 (D5688) was photographed at Skew Bridge with a train from Valley Sidings. These flasks would have originated from Trawsfynydd Nuclear Power Station, which was decommissioned in 1991 but the trains continued to run until 1997.

Black 5 No. 45025 (10A) was photographed on the Down fast at Farington with 3P04, the 09.30 Manchester Victoria to Blackpool North Parcels. It is passing the site of Farington station (opened on 31 October 1838 and closed on 7 March 1960) with the East Lancs LYR line bridge in the background and beyond that Croston Road (originally known as Farington Lane) Bridge from which the station was accessed by prospective passengers. The original ELR curve joined the NUR just the other side of the bridge/station location but back in 1844 the railway crossed the road on the same level.

By 1971 the Class 50s had put in high mileages on the WCML. This busy scene at Farington Junction sees Nos 436 and 439 in charge of 1M18, the 07.20 Glasgow Central to London Euston on 29 July. Track rationalisation prior to electrification works is in progress. The signal box was closed on 5 November 1972 when control was passed to the new Preston Power Box. The line on the right leads round to Lostock Hall Junction, to which point the electrification works extended. (KDH Archive)

Buckshaw Parkway station was opened on 3 October 2011 and was built very close to the site of the old Chorley ROF station, which closed on 27 September 1965. In conjunction with the electrification of the lines between Manchester and Preston/Blackpool Northern Rail received forty-three Class 331 EMU sets built by CAF in Spain. Three-car set No. 331010 is seen on 2 September 2022 leading 1Y56, the 08.59 Blackpool North to Manchester Airport.

Engineering Works were taking place on the WCML south of Preston on 1 November 1992. Consequently, the 10.00 London Euston to Glasgow Central was diverted via Manchester and is seen with Class 47 No. 47522 (D1105) *Doncaster Enterprise* piloting Class 87 No. 87009 *City of Birmingham* at Stump Lane. Chorley station is in the background. The caravan trading site was still going strong in 2024.

When the Class 150/1 DMUs were first introduced in 1985 they were turned out in this attractive two-tone blue-and-white Provincial livery, which was the reverse of the Class 150/2 livery. Set No. 150109 was photographed on 17 March 1990 departing Chorley with a Blackpool North to Nottingham service. (Martyn Hilbert)

A pair of Class 101 DMUs with set No. 101677 comprising car Nos 51496 and 51179 leading is seen departing Chorley station on 13 June 1992 with the 09.55 Blackpool North to Manchester Victoria. The set was withdrawn from service c. November 1993. The gas holder in the centre dated from the mid-1900s and was dismantled in 2019, while the storage tanks on the right are situated in the Pilkington Oils' depot compound.

Bibliography and Sources

Dakres, Jack, *The Last Tide, A History of the Port of Preston 1886–1981* (Carnegie Press, 1986)
Mills, Chris, *Preston Docks – Reflections of a Once Busy Lancashire Port* (RSR Publications, 2014)
Parker, Norman, *The Preston & Longridge Railway* (The Oakwood Press, 1972)
Preston Digital Archive

Websites

brdatabase.info
disused-stations.org.uk
prestonstation.org.uk
railcar.co.uk
railwaycodes.org.uk
ribblesteam.org.uk
sixbellsjunction.co.uk